Contents

Artichoke House
George Charman

I first encountered the sketch for 'Artichoke House' while wandering along the purple landing above the Oak Hall in Edward James's family home at West Dean, now West Dean College. The sketch, sandwiched between Salvador Dalí's *Mae West Lips Sofa* (1938) (commissioned by James for Monkton House) and Leonora Carrington's *Sketches of the Sphinx* (1966), firmly locates Artichoke House within the Surrealist idiom that was James's life.

My project started life as an idea for a mould of an object that never existed, taking inspiration from James's original design for 'Artichoke House' and from the mould-making technique of 'shuttering' (wooden planks or strips used as a temporary structure to contain setting concrete) that James employed in the construction of his monumental concrete forms in Xilitla, Mexico. I developed a series of drawings playing on the idea that James's design for 'Artichoke House' was the mould by which Xilitla was cast.

As well as highlighting the role of Edward James as a significant contributor to the history of surrealist architecture, *Artichoke House* aims to explore how the pavilion in its many modes of existence—as idea, image and object—encourages us to see anew. Like its etymological origins,[1] the physical presence of the pavilion is fleeting; carried by the wind, it passes in a moment. What endure are the ideas and images formed out of its existence, which in a sense, is the true life of a pavilion.

Edward James

As well as being a patron of the surrealist art movement, supporting artists such as Salvador Dalí, René Magritte and Leonora Carrington, James was also a published poet producing eleven volumes of poetry between 1938 and 39, including *The Bones of My Hand* (1938) under his own James Press. These volumes were admired more for their typography than their content and received little in the way of critical acclaim. Perhaps as a result of a bruised ego, James's later ventures into Surrealist prose, including *So Far So Glad* (1938) were penned under a number of pseudonyms including Edward Silence, Edward Selsey and, later, Edward Vayarta.

James's only novel, *The Gardener Who Saw God* (1937) faired better with the critics and was published in England and America to favourable reviews. The text was inspired by a vision James had in the spring of 1935 while sitting alone for dinner in the family dining room at West Dean. He describes a vast sphere of light forming above his head turning faster and faster as Beethoven's *Eroica* symphony began to fill the room. Within this sphere of light were all the plants and trees spread out according to their genuses and all the animals ordered according to their species. (see page 14-15) Running from the dining room clutching his head, James collapsed to the floor and was found moments later by his butler in a semi-conscious state of confusion. This hallucination, commencing as it did with an aura of light around the head, could be suggestive of a classical migraine. Particularly intense migraine attacks can induce vivid hallucinations; sufferers may see human figures, animals, faces, objects or landscapes often multiplied and distorted in size and shape. The writer Lewis Carroll was a sufferer of intense migraine attacks, leading to the suggestion that his migraine experiences may have been the inspiration for the strange alterations of size and shape in *Alice In Wonderland* .[2]

One could argue that this hallucinatory episode, as well as spawning his most successful literary endeavour, was a touchstone for many of James's subsequent explorations into Surrealism, particularly Surrealist architecture.

James initiated his ventures into the realm of Surrealist architecture with the overhaul of his home, Monkton House. Originally built by Edwin Lutyens for Edward's father, William, in 1902, as a hunting lodge on the grounds of West Dean Estate, Monkton House was transformed by James into a Surrealist hermitage. In addition to bamboo-inspired drain pipes, plaster drapes attached to the exterior of the house appeared to hang from the windows, and exterior non-load bearing columns sculpted from plaster resembled giant tropical ferns.

Following Monkton House, James was approached by the Edwardian Society with a proposition to relocate the feted Edwardian façade of the Pantheon (Oxford Street, London), designed in 1772 by James Wyatt, who also conceived the plans for Edward's family home, to West Dean. James commissioned architect Christopher Nicholson, who also worked on Monkton House, to design a home that incorporated the Pantheon façade, to be situated in the West Dean Estate. Nicholson produced a maquette of the Pantheon, from which artist John Piper designed a scheme for a series of caryatids that were to resemble the monolithic Moai statues of Easter Island. Due to spiraling costs and the onset of war, the project was abandoned. In 1952 the Pantheon stones were destroyed. The original model for the Pantheon now rests on a felt-topped table on the purple landing at West Dean.

On the wall, looking down from an aerial perspective onto this miniaturized version of a building that never was, sits 'Artichoke House'. More specifically, there sits an idea rendered in pencil and watercolour of what 'Artichoke House' might have been had James's vision for the pavilion been realised. Plans for the pavilion, designed to resemble a giant globe artichoke, were conceived by James and developed with Christopher Nicholson and Sir Hugh Casson in 1936 as a gallery to house a sample of James's extensive collection of Surrealist art. It is unclear why 'Artichoke House' was never realized but most probably, like the Pantheon, the proposed pavilion became a casualty of circumstance.

In the 1970's James designed another pavilion known as 'The Globular Gallery' with British architect John Warren. (see page 42-45)

Sharon-Michi Kusunoki, former archivist of the Edward James Cultural Archive, suggests its form and function as an exhibition space marks a return in James's thoughts to the unrealized desires embodied in the design for 'Artichoke House'.[3] The Globular Gallery, like 'Artichoke House', with its retractable walls that reveal a glass inner shell, may be understood as an attempt to physically manifest James's vision of a sphere of light cradling the wonders of creation. As in previous projects, James's ambition and vision overshot the reality of the cost and logistics of realisation: The Globular Gallery never reached fruition.

In 1944 Edward James left West Dean Estate for the Sierra Madre Mountains in Mexico. Here he would continue his exploration of vegetal inspired architectural forms that began with the design of 'Artichoke House'. During this period, James constructed more than 200 monumental Surrealist pavilions cast in concrete and situated in the remote tropical jungle of Xilitla, inspired by the flora and fauna that surrounded him there. Within this tropical wilderness James's imagination took flight.

In a letter, the poet William Blake declared *'to the eye of the man of imagination, nature is imagination itself'*.[4] Xilitla was for James an attempt to fuse together his unconscious , as manifested in the monumental concrete forms he produced, with the raw natural landscape that engulfed him. One could argue that this is what James had been attempting for most of his life, shifting the constructs of the familiar in search of something closer to his true nature.

J. G. Ballard, a writer who followed the Surrealists in believing the world could be remade by the human mind, details in *The Unlimited Dream Company* (1979) a succession of surreal images held together by a single landscape. Ballard chose to unravel this rhapsodic vision, suffused with *'flamingos and frigate-birds, falcons and deep-water albatross'* ,[5] in the sleepy suburban town of Shepperton on the outskirts of London, where he lived from 1960 until his death in 2009.

Shepperton was in many ways as alien to Ballard, who had grown up in Shanghai during the Second World War, as Xilitla was to James. Like Xilitla, Shepperton offered Ballard a landscape akin to the

sensibilities of his imagination; a transmutable topography shaped
by unfettered human desire. Ballard's protagonist in *The Unlimited
Dream Company*, not accidentally named Blake, is a character led by his
imagination, an outsider between worlds searching for a place where his
true nature could take root. He describes himself as a:

*'Rejected would-be mercenary pilot, failed Jesuit novice, unpublished
writer of pornography ... yet for all these failures I had a tenacious faith in
myself, a messiah as yet without a message who would one day assemble
a unique identity out of this defective jigsaw.'* [6]

One could argue that Xilitla was James's 'defective jigsaw', constructed
from an amalgam of images, thoughts and dreams crystalized in
concrete, forming a type of architectural mandala. At its centre,
surrounded by a concrete cast of misfits, James was attempting to plot
his place in the universe. Xilitla could thus be seen as James's bid to
express what Jung referred to as the 'active imagination', where one
enters the fantasy of the psyche through a state of reverie, becoming an

active participant in the drama through a process of creative expression, manifest, in James's case, in the architectural forms he produced.

Jung's own architectural mandala was a stone tower built to his specifications beside the upper lake at Bollingen, Zurich, where he accomplished his most important works both on himself and in his study of psychology. Similarly I see 'Artichoke House' as both the manifestation of reverie and as a room for dreaming. In many ways, *Artichoke House*, situated in the grounds of West Dean, will exist in both the past and the future, encompassing elements of an idea that spawned Xilitla, arguably the most important example of Surrealist architecture, and as a re-imagined surreal space built as a platform to explore mobile states of thought and feeling.

At the end of his life Jung wrote:

"At Bollingen I am in the midst of my true life, I am most deeply myself". [7]

Artichoke House (2014)

Artichoke House is a dwelling in the half-light between the real and the fantastical, where reverie becomes the catalyst for creation.   Re-imagining this surreal proposition is also about exploring the fluid back-and-forth relationship between image and object that was as integral to the way James approached the creative process as it is for my own way of working.

As for Edward James, drawing for me too marks the beginning of possibility. The act of drawing brings thought into being and, in a sense, the idea reaches a type of completion. The shift from two-dimensions to three-dimensions is brought about by the existence of the drawing, which is also the beginning of a new set of concepts and propositions independent from its origins. The fact that James's design for 'Artichoke House' never made that shift from 2D image to 3D object allowed me the freedom to rethink the context in which the pavilion would both operate and be experienced.

Less grandiose in its appearances than James's design, resting on its side, *Artichoke House* appears to sink into the ground like a geodesic dome that has grown additional protuberances to its spherical form. Its lopsided profile is suggestive of the ephemeral nature of built things, destined like James's concrete pavilions in the Mexican jungle to inevitably fall into ruin and become subsumed by the environment that cradles it, leaving in its absence, images for the future.

Originally intended by James as a vessel to support images of the surreal, *Artichoke House* and its camera obscura, support a different kind of image, one that alludes to the past, relative to its specific location, but is always operating in a reversed present.

Born from this optical somersault, *Artichoke House* becomes an inhabitable eye through which the visual can be reinterpreted. This dynamic image within the object completes a type of organic loop from image to object and back again. The surface of the object becomes a platform for the development of new images that in turn will form new objects.

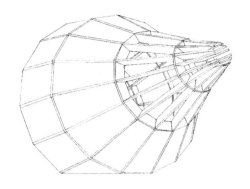

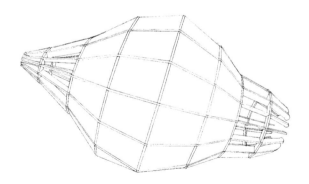

Artichoke House 2014: plan drawings
George Charman

'I suddenly saw the room begin to spin. I looked up at the celling and I saw – I knew it was a projection of my unconscious – but I saw a circle of all of creation with a great light in the middle, and all the flowers and trees according to their geneses spread out, and all of the animals according to their races and families all around this central light. The circle began to turn faster and faster as the music of the last movement of Beethoven's *Eroica* symphony seemed to fill the room.'

Both in Progress: Artichoke House and a Typology
of Sculpture
A Dialogue between Marsha Bradfield and Lucy Tomlins

Marsha Bradfield and Lucy Tomlins are the Directors of Pangaea
Sculptors' Centre (PSC), a new London-based resource to support
artists and others in their practice of sculpture and 3D art.
www.pangaeasculptorscentre.com

Marsha Bradfield

Let me start by saying that we'll take up George Charman's *Artichoke House* by looping through time, moving both forwards and backwards as we try to understand where the project came from and wager where it may be going. I'm slightly uncomfortable with this speculative approach but then again, maybe its apt, as at the time of this conversation, the pavilion aspect of the project has not yet been realised.

Lucy Tomlins

I think I understand your discomfort. It's a bit like the difference between a drawing—a sketch—for building something and that same something, *built*. There's always a difference between these states of being. But it's not until the thing has shifted from being on paper to being an object that you can really grasp what that difference is.

MB   But the nice thing about engaging *Artichoke House* at this stage in its development is that we have very good grounds for sidestepping any reference to the 'finished' project's reception. It's a 'known unknown' at the time of composing this dialogue. In the event that when it's read, this 'known unknown' has become a 'known known', it goes without saying the relation between this text here and Charman's project out there could only be roughly predicted in advance.

LT   In other words, the difference between theory and practice.

MB   Yes. Now something else to mention at the onset of this dialogue relates to the popularity of so-called 'parallel texts' like this one. They're favored in curatorial publications as a kind of 'writing around' for creating context. 'Writing around' something, in this case *Artichoke House*, helps to provide a side story as a kind of variation on a backstory, if you will. I like the idea of this parallel text, our dialogue that is, anticipating the pavilion that occasioned it without attempting to represent *Artichoke House*, if you see what I mean.

So with that established, it's an opportune moment to mention our shared interest, which is to say Pangaea Sculptors' Centre's particular interest in *Artichoke House*. This immediate dialogue is part of an ongoing conversation we've been having as we try to identify different types of sculpture—a typology of sculpture, so to speak. So it's from this broader discussion that we're asking the question: What can *Artichoke House* tell us about how sculpture is currently typologised and what might this ordering reveal about Charman's project?

LT   Of course materials have played a key role in the categorisation of sculpture. We can think of bronze, metal, wooden sculpture, cast rubber, readymades, etc. And then there are art historical divisions: figurative; abstract; kinetic; representational; realist; planar, by which I mean the form has a modeled or carved surface in contrast to being stereometric. This is when the internal structure is exposed.[1] 'Installation' was more recently added to the list, with it being part-sculpture, part-built environment. Sometimes installations offer an immersive experience in the spirit of a *Gesamtkunstwerk*, with the artwork bringing together many art forms into an architecture of material and other relations.

MB   Speaking of which, there's also socially engaged practice in general and relational aesthetics in particular, to throw into the sculptural mix, with the latter being described as not so much 'a theory of art but as a theory of form'—or formations—which strikes me as a sculptural preoccupation.[2]

LT   Because it's about the relationship between 'things' that are often physical, whether this is stuff, space or people?

MB   Precisely. But the really interesting thing about relational aesthetics for me is that this loosely knit body of practice (we can think of work by Vanessa Beecroft and Rirkrit Tiravanija, among others) is actually preoccupied with social formations: inter-subjective exchange— people in relation to each other.[3] It's not about the phenomenological experience of an object in a space—nothing like Minimalism, if you see what I mean.
      Something similar to this non-object-oriented emphasis is also going on in Joseph Beuys' praxis of 'social sculpture', which is about transforming society; that's its use value. Everyone is an artist and together we can sculpt social practices, habits, customs, laws and other institutions, organisations and environments—you name it. 'Even

peeling a potato can be a work of art as long as it is a conscious act'.[4] It's not exactly stone carving but it's still a sculptural practice when it's about critically and creatively reproducing the world as the greatest work of art—the ultimate *Gesamtkunstwerk*.

LT   How about growing an artichoke? That seems more appropriate given the form of Charmans's project. But in all seriousness, the problem with such an elastic definition is that it makes sculpture everything and nothing and that's not very helpful. Hopefully, by putting this art form in the critical crosshairs and typologising current practice in relation to sculptural tradition, we'll rouse its self-consciousness a bit. Yes this is about how sculpture sculpts the world in weird and wonderful ways. But it's also about how the world sculpts sculpture. So there's reciprocity there.

MB   Okay so let's hold onto that idea and keep the typology as something this dialogue will feed into—eventually. Bringing this back to George Charman, I'd like to say a bit more about the ideological dimension of sculpture as a way of making sense and exploring the world. I'm really thinking about the historical avant-garde's drive to fuse art and life that marked Surrealism, and hence Surrealist sculpture, because it seems an important locus of meaning in Charman's approach to *Artichoke House*—or at least as a point of departure.

So Charman tells the story of wandering through West Dean College, formally the ancestral home of Edward James, which sounds like a bit of a Surrealist *Gesamtkunstwerk* in its own right but I've never been there myself. Anyway, James was a prolific patron of Surrealism and an acclaimed Surrealist architect to boot, though it seems his poetry was less successful. In any event, it was while touring West Dean that Charman encountered James's design for his unrealised pavilion *Artichoke House*. It's a good image: Charman contemplating the framed drawing hung between Salvador Dali's *Mae West Lips Sofa* and Leonora Carrington's *Sketches of the Sphinx*. And similarly the other thing to say about Charman's *Artichoke House*, with this being inspired by James's design, is that these iterations make meaning through relation.

LT   Yes I can see that. But how does Surrealism feature in Charman's project beyond, that is, being an historical reference—or a point of departure?

MB   Well I suppose it could be argued that if 'making strange' is what drives Surrealism, with this being a process of re-presenting the familiar so that we see it less habitually and hence can embrace its irrational aspects or dimensions, I suppose Charman's sketches of *Artichoke House* may have a similar effect on James's design, prompting us to see it differently. Of course, James's work has historical priority as both a concept and an object, or objects (sketches) that precede and inspire Charman's project. But it's still unclear how this ontological relation will play out.

LT   And especially since Charman has made his own architectural sketches for the pavilion that will be realised in 2014 as part of his residency at West Dean. Don't you think there's something interesting in the interpretive role that drawing plays in Charman's practice?

MB   It's a good point because the artworks featured on his website are largely drawing-based.[5] George makes representations of three-dimensional spaces—built environments that are uninhabited, leaving them lonely and quiet. Encountering these drawings in the non-place of the Internet, I can't help feeling melancholy as I project myself into their visionary architecture. Of course, I know I'm experiencing the drawings as screen-based reproductions. If I encountered them in the hang of an exhibition, I might well be drawn into a wealth of detail, which gets flattened through their digitisation. Yet what lingers for me is the sense impression of their spatial proposition. I feel dislocated when recollecting the drawings in my mind's eye. This spatial awareness is something I often associate with sculpture and it's clear Charman is an artist with sculptural tendencies, even while he's working on a flat surface. But this isn't the same thing as being a sculptor per se.

LT   So it might be interesting to spin this on its head. You've been talking about the role of sculpture in Charman's practice as essentially drawing-based. But what about the role that drawing plays in a sculptural project like *Artichoke House*? I'm thinking about something that sculptor Grenville Davey said recently when he spoke to us about his own sculptural sensibility. So Davey talked about drawing being the place where things start to really work for him, which explains why he's making drawings all the time. There is this really interesting idea that some things seem impossible to make but then you work them up as drawings and they're kind of made already. That's the moment when he goes to the material and starts shifting the sculpture from being on paper and in theory to a materialised object in practice.[6]

To take this further, Charman's sketches suggest that he might be using the sculptural structure itself in the same way as a draughtsman uses a sketch or illustration to propose something *other*, something yet to be. Of course, I'm projecting now onto the unknown and we said we'd stay out of that territory, but I'm wondering whether Charman's *Artichoke House* might end up operating as a three-dimensional sketch, or proposition rather than trying to embody the something 'other' in its essence?

MB So, if I understand correctly, you're making a distinction between speculative, sculptural illustration of something 'other' in a sketch and the embodiment of something 'other' in the sculptural object? Are you suggesting these could be different types in our sculpture typology?

LT Yes perhaps. Although there are plenty of artists whose approaches bleed across the two, so it might be that the positions bookend a sliding scale. To illustrate, we could put an Ikea showroom at one end of the spectrum and a real home, kitted out with Ikea furniture, at the other. They both use the same materials; they look the same in many respects. But the first is an 'image', a projection of an idea, and the second has a truth to materials and an embodiment of a 'lived in' truth. Water runs through its pipes, wrinkles on the sheets tell an historic narrative.

An artist like Manfred Pernice is interesting to throw into the mix here.[7] I'm thinking specifically of works such as *Que-Sah*. Here he combines found objects and surfaces, made from materials like tile or particleboard, with ones he's created or had created for exhibition. It's a bit odd because it can be difficult to know where the installation begins or ends, as it seems to reach out and incorporate the areas around it.

Nevertheless, the ideas in play often emphasise the experience of the constructed space, which could be the gallery, the departure lounge or the Ikea showroom.

The idea of the constructed space butts up against Charman's *Artichoke House* in his description of its function as a pavilion. It will be interesting to see where it plays out on this spectrum. Given his background in drawing, I am speculating, perhaps incorrectly, it may be closer to the Ikea showrooom—closer to an image of an ideal. Charman has also talked about temporariness of the structure (it will be moved), which is interesting when we think about its construction in concrete-clad timber. Though maybe with the added ingredient of time, in the existence of the realised object, *Artichoke House* will move back along the scale; away from sketch of something 'other' towards an identity and visible history of its own.

MB You know the pavilion in James's sketches looks a lot like a rocket. It's in the shape of a globe artichoke that appears ready for blastoff—ready to take us to another dimension. It's a curious case of form following function because the pavilion was initially conceived as an exhibition space for James's collection of Surrealist artworks. And no doubt the experience would have been out of this world.

Now what Charman envisions in his sketches is quite different from this—it's something closer to a globe light set on its side, which is also poignant if we're thinking about form following function because in this case, the pavilion will house a camera obscura. It will have the surreal effect of using a lens and natural light to visualise the pavilion's surroundings as an image projected upside down on an interior wall. So there is a very strong visual aspect of *Artichoke House* that runs right through its development—from James's sketches as an historical and stylistic point of departure to Charman's own drawings for a pavilion that will features a camera obscura.

LT The pavilion will also act as a spatio-visual interruption to the usual landscape of West Dean—it's a reference point to the narrative history running throughout the gardens and house and the stories of Edward James.

MB This seems a good point to go back to your question, Lucy: What can *Artichoke House* tell us about how sculpture is currently typologised and what might this ordering perhaps reveal about Charman's project? I think drawing, photography—the visual—seems to be leading *Artichoke House*. It's like there are these various bits and pieces but common to them all is this vegetal visual.

When it comes to how Charman's *Artichoke House* sits in our typology, I think it depends on its visual form. It's less about material, ideology, social concerns, historical precedent or even space and more about how we see *Artichoke House* and what it prompts us to see.

LT Yes but if I can add to that, and I think this is important, what makes the project sculptural in contrast to architectural is the priority that Charman places on the evolution and development of the pavilion and its form as it shifts between states of being—from sketch to object, to inhabitable space, etc.

Let me explain what I mean by this with reference to something that artist Luke Jerram said when Pangaea Sculptors' Centre interviewed him (at the time of writing we're in the edit stage of a video that describes the sculptural sensibility of his practice). Jerram keyed into a refrain in discussions about British sculpture today: We've got to take more risks.[8] It's something that Richard Wilson has tried to impress upon us too.[9] But Jerram's point is that it's not just about taking risk. It's also about how an artist handles or responds to failure that separates the successful from the less successful.[10] So perhaps the separation between the sculptural and the architectural also involves recognition of the potential of risk and a positive position on the states of insecurity and uncertainty that go hand in hand with this.

As is often the case today, and is certainly the case with *Artichoke House*, the opportunity to take risk, in so far as creating ambitious three-dimensional work is concerned, is tied up with its being commissioned and thus public, due to the cost of realisation. Though because it's sponsored by a third-party organisation or funder, there is a rub that needs to be managed by the artist between their desire for risk and experimentation and their understanding that in the mind of the supporter, it cannot fail or be seen as a failure.

MB But the fact of the matter is that a significant aspect of *Artichoke House* is the pavilion and its site specificity. Even if it could be physically resolved in the studio beforehand, how it shows up in the dialogue with the site can be considered but cannot be entirely predicted until it's there, in situ. So back to 'known unknowns'. But where does that leave us with the typology?

LT Well I like this idea of the visual leading the project and the pavilion iterating and being transformed over the course of its development. In the case of *Artichoke House* we can trace this at least as far back as James's own surreal sketches, born of his equally surreal impulse to realise a built environment in the shape of an edible thistle. No doubt this historical backstory helps to contextualise the project, as will the pavilion's site-specificity at West Dean. But I sense a more radical possibility for *Artichoke House*'s significance, as a sculptural enterprise, isn't dependent on these external references at all. This isn't because the pavilion fancies itself as somehow autonomous or ahistorical. It's because as a project, *Artichoke House* prioritises the pavilion—a pavilion, moreover, that's built instead of speculatively illustrating something imaginary. And it's because it's built that we're able to enjoy a different kind of phenomenological encounter with the project that's distinct from when we encounter the sketches—or how they encounter the proposition. I think this encounter is at the project's core and I'm looking forward to the experience of *Artichoke House* as an object in the landscape of West Dean.

MB It will also be interesting to see how this meshes with viewing the same landscape inside the pavilion, the visuals made by the camera obscura. Of course it makes sense to experience *Artichoke House* before we locate it and the project more generally in our typology of sculpture. But let me share something in closing that sprang to mind when you were emphasising the importance of encountering the pavilion as built. So there's this figure in James's original sketches—included for scale, presumably. I read him as a self-portrait of James, who looks awfully pleased for a man who failed to bring his plans for the pavilion to fruition. Now the same figure also appears in some of Charman's sketches. Only here, James is as white as a ghost. These references make me think about the project's visuals in another way. James may haunt *Artichoke House* but Charman's project isn't about fulfilling the architect's vision. It's instead about reviewing and renewing a surreal proposition in a more concrete form, however temporary and site specific. I too look forward to encountering *Artichoke House* as both an image and a structure and thinking more, then, about how its nexus of visual/built/iteration/proposition/embodiment might sit in our sculptural typology.

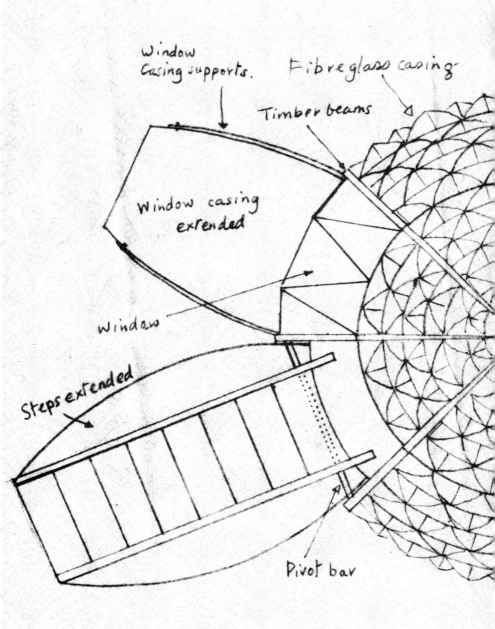

Window
Casing supports.

Fibreglass casing.

Timber beams

Window casing
extended

Window

Steps extended

Pivot bar

$\frac{1}{2}" = 1'$

Concrete Foundations

Steel supports for main structure

Bracing plates

Main foundation steel struts

Plan for Artichoke Pavilion.

Edward James and the Poetry of the Imagination
Sharon-Michi Kusunoki

Dr Sharon-Michi Kusunoki is a curator, lecturer and art historian. As part of the research for her doctorate, Dr Kusunoki located, amalgamated and organised a mass of fragmented correspondence creating what is now known as The Edward James Cultural Archive. She has contributed to several international publications and has lectured and written extensively on Edward James and Surrealism. She is currently working on an anthology of the letters of Edward James.

'When I was a child I used to have the most extraordinary surrealist fantasies. I think one of the reasons that my fantasy was developed so intensely was that I was forced to rest quite unnecessarily, when I should have been allowed to run around in the garden. I was made to sleep in my perambulator, and I couldn't sleep ... I remember ... a wonderful fine day in August, sun pouring through the blinds at seven.

I wanted to get out of my little bed, but I was hemmed in by big brass rails ... I wasn't allowed to [get up] until Nanny woke up ... So ... I would have to invent a world, and therefore all my blankets became a flying city, and I made domes out of the pillows, and I would get under it and imagine that I was in a series of halls, and this was Aladdin's palace flying over the world.' [1]

In the 1930s Edward James emerged from a painful and disastrous marriage to the Viennese ballet dancer, Tilly Losch, and began to immerse himself in what appeared to be a quest to put the images of his imagination into concrete form. His work celebrated the emotive and aesthetic qualities of architecture without concern for functionality or indeed, practicality. His watercolour design for 'Artichoke House' was found in a suitcase in a warehouse in Los Angeles in the early 1980s. Inside this suitcase were cocoons of tissue paper from which emerged a mass of fragments of correspondence. Surprisingly, these fragments appeared to have been either systematically disorganised, or arranged following the 'laws of chance' rather than reason. From their tissue paper shrouds tumbled page 2 of one letter, page 5 of another, most often without dates or any indication as to whom the letter was written.

Piecing together Edward James's archive was like piecing together a jigsaw puzzle containing over 300,000 colourful pieces. To follow traditional archival methods would have been futile and unnecessarily time-consuming, for his archive was a game with undisclosed rules. The suitcases and trunks were the game-board, and the fragments of correspondence, of which the drawing of the 'Artichoke House' was one, made up the pieces—small treasures cast at random in an act of play. The archivist, robbed of the formal language of conventional taxonomy, is forced to move from the condition of observer to that of active participant in order to complete what has now become a creative process aimed at the restructuring of meaning. Hence, the archivist must devise a set of rules framed by intended use, and his or her own view of reality. Chance is a factor as is surprise, for as the archivist carefully unwraps each layer of tissue paper, packets of sugar, or sometimes drawings by Salvador Dalí or René Magritte, are randomly unveiled.

In his archives, James forces a reordering of the visible world through a revision of objective form, a paradox we see explored in the drawing of the 'Artichoke House,' arguably a pavilion that was meant to be a gallery to house James's growing 'collection' of art. (see page 34-35)

'I never set out with a view to making any 'collection'... a word which has never appealed to me ... it seems to indicate entirely the wrong attitude towards art. A true patron of artists is mainly interested in promoting talent and not ... with a view to self-aggrandizement ... my so-called 'collection'... has already served its prime and initial purpose both by assisting financially and encouraging morally young painters at a time when they most needed encouragement at the incipience of their careers.'[2]

Although the watercolour drawing of the 'Artichoke House' is undated, it is thought to have originated in the 1930s when James was working on a number of projects for Monkton House, the house originally designed by Sir Edwin Lutyens on James's family estate. By 1935 James was in the process of transforming Monkton into a Surrealist hermitage. Not unlike the efforts of William Beckford[3] and Horace Walpole[4] to reshape the English country house, Edward James attempted to resynthesize Lutyens, to create a new façade for the house, encasing his pipes and painting them green to resemble bamboo, and placing plaster swags and draperies under a mock Queen-Anne arts-and-crafts type of decorative style

With its padded walls and neo-classical crosses, the dining room is a travesty of 18th-century taste (see page 31), whilst in the tunnel-like hall on the first floor, James installed mirrors or hung paintings by Leonor Fini giving a sense of infinity at each end of the hall. Through his designs and experimentation, James developed an eclecticism that pulled together past, present and the world of fantasy in a coherent and effective way.

Two years after the watercolour design for the 'Artichoke House' was found in Los Angeles, a sketch for its interior was uncovered in a suitcase located in the Tower Suite of Edward James's home in England.

This sketch indicated that a fibreglass sheath was to be used in the building, in turn suggesting that the drawing and sketch may have been initiated by Christopher Nicholson, the architect with whom James was working in the late 1930s, but then completed at a later date by Nicholson's partner, Sir Hugh Casson. In a letter from Casson dated 14 December 1939, Casson indicates that he is enclosing copies of plans concerning Monkton House, but as the office is closed, he no longer has the means with which to finish colouring them.[5]

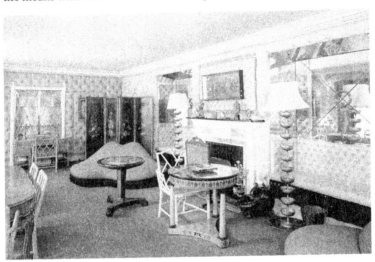

As referred to earlier, it is thought that the 'Artichoke House' was meant to be a pavilion intended as a gallery to house some of James's art. This is supported by a later development, when James asked the British architect, John Warren, to design The Globular Gallery in the 1970s. (see page 44-45) Both designs are similar in shape and purpose, with the windows of the imagination opened in a seeming inversion of the natural enclosure of a gallery. As in the drawing of the 'Artichoke House', where the leaves are hinged so that they can fall away from the core, the paintings in the transparent Globular Gallery were to be mounted facing inwards so that the viewer would be able to see the paintings against the surrounding landscape and outside light. Five storeys high, The Globular Gallery was to be set in the centre of a circular lake at the front of James's West Dean House with a cylindrical fish tank at its centre, around which wound a spiral staircase.[6] However, due to the cost of erecting this structure, this project never reached fruition.

Edward James's original idea for sectioning the windows of his pavilion is interesting, especially as it developed at the time when Walt Disney's first animated feature film was released.[7] James's design allows the spectator to experience the inner space and James's collection of art against the constant transformation of the landscape beyond. As in some of the work of James's great friend, René Magritte, James blurred the boundary between interior and exterior space. His collection of paintings, projected on to the changing landscape, suggests a re-representation of that which exists and, as in animation, the resulting images create a sense of fluid motion.

This element of motion is also present in George Charman's interpretation, where the external landscape is projected, via a camera obscura, into its interior. In Charman's piece, the pavilion is toppled yet there is a platform for spectators to enter as if they were actors on a stage. Although sited within the opulence of the gardens of James's family estate, Charman's piece is pluralistic, a wink at an aristocratic hierarchy which appears structurally solid, but is presented as an ornamental ruin. Like the society that it can be said to represent, the cladding of the walls of the structure ensures insularity. The viewers are on the one hand privileged, isolated and contained—loiterers, as James might say— on the plinth of a fallen monument. At the same time, the viewers are encouraged to look outside to discover the truth. The presence of the camera obscura is significant, as it serves as a tool to project and record new realities simultaneously as the spectator not only views, but is also allowed to escape into, and become part of, the space beyond. (see page 12-13)

The idea of immersing oneself in the beauty of the landscape is an ideology to which James himself subscribed. Indeed, in what was intended as the preface for his proposed book, *The First Volume*, James wrote:

It can be argued that Edward James's 'Artichoke House' is the precursor of the organic forms he built in Las Pozas, the 'Garden of Eden' he created in the jungles near Xilitla, Mexico between 1947 and 1984. His exploration of the effect of light on the structural principles of shape, form, rhythm, volume and colour, evident in his design for the 'Artichoke House,' are also principles apparent in his structures in Las Pozas, where James seemed to respond to the environment without concerning himself with the functions that might be required. Again, there were precedents for James's work, most especially in the Royal Pavilion in Brighton where a classical English villa is transformed by changing the exterior into a palace based on Indian architectural forms. Like James's creations in Xilitla, the Royal Pavilion is, in a sense, an opening of a dream-like fantasy world of decadent aesthetics.

Whilst George Charman's interpretation of the 'Artichoke House' is built as an enclosure, Edward James's structures in Las Pozas illustrate a bid for freedom. A cinematographic space of simultaneous perceptions—cinemas without walls, buildings without roofs, a dialectic tension between inside and outside and the rational and the creative that followed James throughout his life.

Las Pozas consists of 17 acres of a 75-acre semi-tropical jungle-clad hillside that James purchased in the Sierra Madre Mountains near Xilitla in Mexico in 1947/8. From this time forward, James used the landscape as a canvas on which to create his 'Garden of Eden,' a world of over 200 vibrantly coloured cement structures that whilst architectural in character, were highly sculptural, poetic and without regard to the normal limitations of architecture, the tenet that form should follow function. Importing a collection of over 20,000 orchids as well as deer, ocelots, parrots and other birds, James's jungle retreat began to resemble the overgrown Aztec city visited by the artist, Max Ernst, in his dreams, as well as highlighting an obvious connection between Ferdinand Cheval's Ideal Palace, [9] and the hallucinatory vision of creation that James had had while dining in his West Dean home. (see page 14-15)

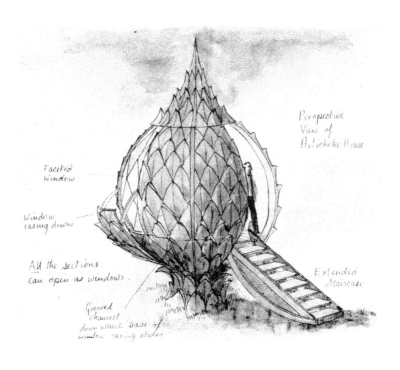

Perspective
View of
Artichoke House

Faceted
Window

Window
casing down

All the sections
can open as windows.

Grooved
Channel
down which base of
window casing slides

Extended
Staircase

Christopher Nicholson
Watercolour sketch of the exterior of 'Artichoke House' (circa 1930's)
Edward James Cultural Archive

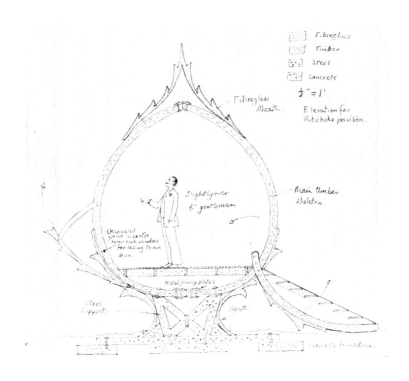

Fibreglass
Timber
Steel
Concrete

½" = 1'

Elevation for
Artichoke pavilion.

Fibreglass
Sheath.

Slightly over
6' gentleman

Main timber
skeleton

Channeled
groove in center
below each window
for casing to run
down.

Metal joining plates

Steel
Supports

Sheath

Concrete foundations

Christopher Nicholson / Sir Hugh Casson
Design for the interior of 'Artichoke House' (circa 1930's)
Edward James Cultural Archive

In Las Pozas James began by creating structures that had obvious illusions to the past, particularly to Italian and Continental architecture. However, as he matured his style changed and he responded to his environment with a spontaneity and wit that used the forms of nature, and the strength of architecture, to create a surreal city that celebrated the hidden aspects of the marvellous ... buildings with stairs that go up and then catapult the climber off the edge of a platform three storeys high ... rooms without walls, houses shaped like whales, brightly coloured flora made out of steel-reinforced concrete, a synchronicity between colour, vegetation and form.

In the past, Edward James had admired the work of Antoni Gaudí, whose architecture Salvador Dalí once described as:

'simultaneously Utopian and archaic, mystical and sensuous, Catalan and universal, humble and megalomaniac, gothic and baroque, a secret pivot of modernity by virtue of its very contradictions.' [10]

As suggested by Leonora Carrington in her novel *The Stone Door*, these elements are also present in Las Pozas. Carrington, having been inspired by Xilitla after a holiday with James, describes a house she saw during her visit:

In the heart of a deep forest, as black and luxurious as the hair of an Aztec priest, rose a great dwelling. A dwelling Victorian in style, sinister and stubbornly neo-Gothic, Greek as well with, here and there, a few Roman corners, as if the architect had wanted to take a terrible revenge on the period in which he studied ... When it rained, humidity surrounded the house and clung to the walls until a heap of fungi, with colours ranging from orange to green and from purple to sepia, disguised each square centimetre of masonry, giving the bizarre impression that the house was covered with a carapace like a dragon's skin ...' [11]

Like Edward James's ideas for the ever-changing landscape of the 'Artichoke House,' Las Pozas is a place of perpetual transformation and discovery. The complex of the infinite that James once described as 'something that pursues him, which underlies all his poetry'[12] is visible. Within what the American art dealer, Julian Levy, described as the trappings of the nostalgia and romance of the Neo-Romantics, James's creations in Las Pozas play with the notions of ruins and feelings of melancholy, enigma, loss and quiet questioning. They are scattered around the Xilitlan landscape as edifices enveloped or pierced by nature, much like Claude Lorrain's, Nicholas Poussin's and Salvator Rosa's depictions of mock ruins in their landscapes:

There is an air of prefabricated ruin about Edward James's architecture. It is as if he built in order to abandon, but at the same time abandoned in order to build.'[13]

Las Pozas, like many of James's projects, was never completed as his imagination never stopped working. It is not known what James intended for the future of Las Pozas. From the date when he first began building in Xilitla, James amended his Will several times, but never did he make provision for the preservation of his structures. He always thought that they would be subsumed by the surrounding vegetation. But this was not a problem for him, as for James, ruins should be discovered, found as if without warning, buried under the heavy secrets of their past. Indeed, when he visited the Mayan ruins in Chichén Itzá, he wrote in a letter to Leonora Carrington that he went in the back way:

'through a thick covert of brush and underwood, under a barbed wire fence, not to avoid paying my two pesos entrance fee, but to take Chichén Itzá by surprise, which I did.'[14]

Edward James once said that if he lived long enough to finish his 'Garden of Eden,' he wished to crown his construction with a pyramid on which would be perched a fibreglass replica of the horse of Leonardo da Vinci. During the day all one would see would be an enormous white horse, but at night, the inside of the horse would light up to reveal giant palm leaves with brightly-coloured birds flying in and out of the horse's body. In an interview with Sir Hugh Casson, his final description of James was as a bird: *'elusive, almost as if he had wings.'*[15]

Not unlike the birds in the final sculpture James wished to produce, the birds, like the man himself, could not be contained within a rigid structure. The narrative of James's life ends as he began, an artist, a creator, a poet flying over the world in Aladdin's palace, making Surrealist dreams more vivid than life. Not unlike his other pursuits, Edward James's creations in Las Pozas were drawn from an ever-changing palette of colours. In c.1951, James wrote of this changing palette in reference to his poetry, but it is just as applicable to the manner in which he left his archive, and indeed, to Las Pozas itself. With an air of expectancy, James's purposefully deconstructed archives, and his creations in Xilitla, both engage and embrace the nostalgia and influences of his past, while actively encouraging new interpretations:

The problem is that this book, which you have opened, has been compiled over nearly half a lifetime, from poems drawn out of the essence of each peculiar occasion, no one the same - and from almost every land I have ever visited. The colours of my palette were changed each time, to meet the shade of the hour. Behold, therefore, a hundred conflicting and utterly disparate states of mind! There is no one subject to link the entirety; no one style; no single intention; no unity of conviction.

'What common denominator has it?' was what I had to ask myself.

'A certain madness, a peculiar anguish of longing and searching seemed to invest the whole. I had already chosen as an epigraph for the foot of the title page a Greek fragment from a papyrus which reads ... And I yearn, and I seek ...' [16]

When Edward James died in 1984, construction in Las Pozas stopped as James's gaze, like the camera obscura, became fixed as if in a continuous read. His deliberately deconstructed archives have been systematically organised, ready to inspire another generation, and the architectural elements that began with the pod of an artichoke have flowered, and its buds of creativity have been opened to reveal a strip of constant animation. As John Milton reminds us in *'Paradise Lost'* the true 'Garden of Eden' can only exist through the poetry of the imagination.

In an early version of Edward James's publication, *Reading into the Picture*, James wrote:

'I am myself all against pandering to the past ... The past gains its dignity from whatever new influence it is having upon the future. When it offers

nothing new for the future to develop it had far better be forgotten ... Art itself becomes pointless unless it is continually re-creating ... A picture, once it has ceased to inspire new pictures, is a dead thing ... Ah, if we could only create today something that might be worth becoming a ruin.' [17]

In 1984, Edward James's British architect was asked to design a memorial tomb for James that was to be erected in St Roche's Arboretum on James's family estate. John Warren designed a broken-down temple as a reconstructed ruin with fallen columns and a slab in the centre under which James's remains were to be placed. (see page 41-43) The cost was prohibitive and all that survived was the idea of a slab. The slab of Cumbrian green slate was lettered by John Skelton. On it is the 'Symbol of Life' with the words:

EDWARD

JAMES

Poet

Edward James's grave
St Roche's Arboretum, West Dean Estate
Designed by John Warren, lettered by John Skelton

Edward James's grave in the Arboretum
John Warren

At short notice I was asked to make a proposal for Edward's grave slab in St Roche's Arboretum. My mind immediately went to a woodland in Ionia, near Pompeiopolis, where some years previously I had stumbled across a small Roman-Greek temple, tumbled apparently by an earthquake, surrounded by ancient olive groves. Its four columns in antis had been thrown down among the fallen masonry. Its lonely surroundings, dappled by tree shadow, were magically timeless. Having survived for nearly two thousand years, it has been gracefully absorbed into the landscape; a lingering artifact, a tangible work of man integrated into the great growing natural world.

There was a wonderful sense of man's absorption into nature. I had much the same sensation when I wondered alone among Edward's creations at Xilitla. In this design I had in mind using the salvaged classical columns, then languishing in store at West Dean, which now give character to the main corridor in the house; and they are perhaps better there than weathering in the Arboretum. The proposal was, I believe, well received by family and friends but foundered on cost and uncertainty as to who would pay. Eventually only the central slab was commissioned.

John Warren is a graduate of Durham University (Kings College). Between 1969 and 1991 he was the architect to The Edward James Foundation and was responsible for the conversion of Edward James's family home into West Dean college.

The Globular Gallery at West Dean

Edward first put this project to me when we were dining at the White Horse [Chilgrove, West Sussex]. The idea emerged as a series of impetuous sudden thoughts which came together as an explosive concept, a pure sphere poised tantalisingly in a circular lake, central to the view from the house, drawing people in by the sheer magic of its geometry. The idea was simply that it would be a piece of Surrealism greater even than any of its contents. Who would be able to resist the lure of a great glass ball floating on a pure reflective circular lake?

It took some effort of the imagination to crystalise the concept. Rising through the centre there was to be a circular glass column filled with water, air bubbling up through it and fish swimming. A gentle circular staircase was to wind round this surreal core. Three discs of floor were intended, each carrying screens on which the pictures of Tchelitchew, Picasso, Magritte and Dalí would be presented. The topmost storey was to be a viewing gallery with an aviary, equipped with couchette seats to allow the visitors to view the stars; and the floor at water level was to accommodate the reception. It was even suggested that the entire structure should revolve. For a few days—a week or two—Edward was enthusiastic, loved the design and was not to be daunted by any difficulty. The agent saw it as several steps too far, even for the long strides of Edward. I made enquiries, which strengthened my doubts about acceptability at planning, and a preliminary analysis of costs consigned the idea to surreal oblivion.

In the early 1940s, the wealthy English poet and Surrealist patron, Edward James, travelled in North Eastern Mexico with a former Army sergeant named Roland McKenzie. They were searching for wild orchids high in the Sierra Huasteca and had stopped to bathe in the Santa Maria River. As James watched, his traveling companion emerged from the water only to be immediately covered by a cloud of blue and yellow butterflies settling upon his wet body. This suitably surrealistic vision affected James profoundly. Not only did it confirm his desire to settle permanently in Mexico, it also underpinned the location of what would be his most ambitious and enduring creation: the concrete structures of his garden of 'Las Pozas', just outside the small town of Xilitla. James would attempt to cultivate orchids here for some twenty years before beginning to build in concrete from 1962, the site expanding until his death in 1984. What is being proposed is that an etymological link to the founding image of the butterfly—both in the Latin *papilionem* and the French *pavillon*—provides a means by which to think about Edward James's jungle creations as the Pavilions of Xilitla.

Pavilions have a complex currency in the practices and discourses of art, design and architecture. As well as definitions concerning free-standing, subsidiary structures, pavilions are also associated with exhibition, leisure and commercial interests. If the pavilion is devoid of a stable 'type', it instead assumes an array of associative qualities: temporary, contingent, ceremonial, ornamental, fantastical, hybrid and so on. Pavilions are changeable, adaptive, and might be seen as peculiarly rhetorical—potent, even "embattled", structures that embody or provide shelter for idiosyncratic views on the world.[1] Often dismissed as frivolous or insubstantial, pavilions nonetheless symbolise a shadow to architecture proper, a minor sideline to the discipline that can take on attributes of radical experimentation that major architecture cannot.[2] The origins of the pavilion in the butterfly wing-shaped shelters of military campaigns soon became absorbed into the aristocracy through its role in Medieval and Renaissance pageantry. Symbolic of power, property and status from the beginning, pavilions became linked to wealthy individuals, appearing in palatial gardens, villa parks and country estates. Modified according to aesthetic taste, such pavilions would provide structure in garden design, places of refuge or shelter from the sun. They would also serve as belvederes, framing specific views or marking routes through open space. Such image- and space-making qualities already suggest something of the pavilion's uneasy relation to divisions between inside and outside, or between natural and manufactured space. Pavilions would soon become established sites of popular recreation and public entertainment. The landscaped parks of the Regency and Victorian eras saw pavilion-types proliferate into lodges, gazebos, menageries, bandstands, follies, conservatories, summer and glass houses, and so on. Pavilion design became ever more elaborate and eclectic, incorporating mixtures of various styles and motifs. Edward James's pavilions in the Mexican jungle owe something to this spirit of 'sampling', as his designs absorbed references to classical and arcane symbols, from Doric columns, spiral staircases, cornucopias, open platforms, gothic arches and mushroom canopies, curlicues and decorative fronds, fake balustrades and buttresses, heraldic emblems, flutes and trefoils, and so on. Such amalgamations are a signature of Las Pozas, as indeed are the blurred boundaries between sculpture and architecture, between house and garden. Not only did James's pavilions embrace ambiguities between interior and exterior, but also between artwork and dwelling.[3]

From the nineteenth century, pavilions became associated with International Exhibitions, Fairs and Festivals. Edward James had direct experience of pavilion-making at New York's 1939 World's Fair through his collaborative relationship with Salvador Dalí. At the very end of a period of sustained patronage of the artist, James was heavily involved in the development of 'The Dream of Venus', a surreal pavilion designed by Dalí and installed at Flushing Meadows in Queens. The creative boundaries of their collaboration are still debated but James certainly served as one of the financial backers for Dalí's subversive vision, which involved mermaids swimming in an aquarium, surreal objects, costumes and sets incorporating his signature motifs: grand pianos, lobsters and mannequins. Yet if James carried over the influence of Dalí's beloved Antoni Gaudí from the experience, his pavilions in Xilitla would certainly not adhere to any commercial display model: they are contemplative rather than mercantile, labyrinthine rather than regimented, inspirational rather than didactic. Yet the pavilion's capacities as a mode of display still seem important. If it is not in relation to commodities, political propaganda, global marketing or kitsch entertainment, what do the pavilions of Las Pozas contain or put on display?

The origins of Las Pozas are rich and recur throughout James's life. The most common sources include Ferdinand Cheval's *Palais Ideal*, built between 1879 and 1912, a source of fascination for André Breton and the Surrealists. James's financial backing of the Watts Towers in Los Angeles also points to sympathy with what might be called 'naive' or 'outsider' art. Yet James came from a cultured (if traditionally so) background, was well travelled and, as inadvertent collector and patron, had been immersed in the art world since his youth.[4] Las Pozas was the culmination of his lifelong desire to establish a sanctuary or refuge; a 'Garden of Eden', however irrational, fantastical or useless it might seem. This image of a fantasy city had first occurred to James during childhood, inspired by an unknown painting on the wall of his night-nursery (christened, according to Margaret Hooks, 'Seclusia'). This walled city would be the focus of escapist dreams, leaving behind the claustrophobia of an Edwardian upbringing.[5] James would later elaborate on his "dream-vision" in *Reading into the Picture*, a poetic text published in 1936. He speculated at length upon Seclusia's manifold sources—describing it from the outset as a "composite place, never to be located on any map or in any century."[6] This composite nature connects to the melded styles of the pavilions of Las Pozas, as well as confirming the influence of the capriccios or architectural fantasies painted by Hubert Robert or Gustave Moreau. At the same time, James acknowledges his awareness of the Romantic taste for picturesque ruins, referencing the sham versions installed at Potsdam and Versailles, as well as those rendered by Claude Lorrain, Salvator Rosa or Giovanni Piranesi. Yet James's admiration for such "hoary ruins, billowy with ivy, blotted out here and there with festoons of shadow" paled in relation to the possibilities for new structures: "how much more invigorating are new foundations haunted with future hopes and the smell of fresh cement!"[7] Of course, the pavilions of Las Pozas embraced the use of reinforced concrete, which suggests connections not only with industrial design but the archetypal modernist pavilion. Although far from the cool, minimal aesthetic of Mies van der Rohe's Barcelona Pavilion (1923), for example, there are still correlations that can be made: an engagement with experimental materials and form; utopian aspirations; dialogue with openness and transparency; questioning the necessity of walls and ceilings, all conventions of architecture. There is also the attempt to capture spaces in which nature and architecture, garden and sculpture, merge or become difficult to distinguish from one another. But from the belvedere of the Las Pozas pavilions, what do we look out at? Is the viewing position intentionally enfolded, perforated or made complex through the absorption of the unique subjectivity of the architect? Or is it the physical environment? Although James acknowledged the "megalomania" of building such concrete towers, his process was highly collaborative.[8] Alongside his companion and guide Plutarco Gastelum, James worked with local craftsmen to pioneer innovative construction methods that would make his ideas a reality. Wooden formwork would be laboriously crafted for each concrete component—each building being gradually poured into place. Rebar spokes would point from section-ends as if to suggest an unending process. James would work on several structures simultaneously, adding elements as they came to him, more in the spirit of bricolage and improvisation than any considered architectural process.

Even though he was untrained, James had much experience with projects of exterior and interior design. In collaboration with Dalí, he had transformed Monkton House, a hunting lodge on the West Dean estate, turning Edward Lutyen's original design into a Surrealist extravaganza. The array of references feeding into Las Pozas is astounding, suggestive of the pavilion's role as a lens through which cosmopolitan diversity can be focused in one place. In his text on 'Seclusia', James lists various 'models' that, for one reason or another, fell short for his fantasy city: Rothenburg-ob-der-Tauber, a picturesque medieval town in Bavaria; his alma mater the University of Oxford; San Giminiano, a hill town in Tuscany with striking tower houses across its skyline; the elevated city of Perugia; Orvieto, perched on a flat shelf of rock; the fortified towns of Carcassonne and Aigue Morte; Albi and Salzburg. James enthuses about the Spanish city of Toledo, his affection rooted in idealised landscape by El Greco. But as well as real places visited and remembered, James also cited the generic Renaissance City of Paradise, even fantasies like Shangri-la or Xanadu. More interesting, perhaps, are his references to the Palace of Aladdin, made both in *Reading into the Picture* and in an interview from 1978. It is worth noting in relation to Las Pozas that the Genie is instructed to leave the palace unfinished in order that the Sultan may have the honour of completing it.

Given that James remarked: "how often is it the case that either the vegetation or the architecture is disappointing! Seldom are both at their best together," the importance of organic forms in the design of the Las Pozas pavilions cannot be overstated.[9] There is further precedent in James's unrealised project, developed with the architect Sir Christopher Nicholson, for an 'Artichoke Pavilion', a free-standing structure destined for the grounds of West Dean that would present part of James's art collection suspended within a transparent sphere. Already this interest in transparency is suggestive of Xilitla and the modernist pavilion. In another unrealised commission, this time a design for a 'Tower of the Holy Spirit (House for Edward James)' made by Pedro Friedeberg in the early 1960s, an eight-storey structure is topped with a transparent 'aviary' in the form of a dodecahedron, a feature lifted from Leonardo da Vinci's illustrations for Luca Pacioli's early 16th-century treatise, *The Divine Proportion*. One finds similar concerns for transparency, albeit from a different perspective, in the work of American artist Dan Graham, whose pavilion structures become both viewing lenses and performative spaces, blurring the edges between inside and outside. Through the use of two-way mirrors, such that the pavilions become transparent and reflective at the same time, Graham aims to make spectators both subject and object of an immersive experience. Within this there is an inherent critique of the modernist pavilion's claims for the transparency of glass, soon hijacked by corporate opacity, as well as commentary on the technologies of surveillance and the 'blank' spaces of civic architecture (kiosks, bus shelters, foyers, and so on). In the pavilions of Las Pozas, there are alternative images that link to images of other contemporary artists, giving us insight into the projective influence that Xilitla embodies beyond its amalgamation of those of the distant past. If James himself included homages to individual artists such as Max Ernst, Henry Moore, Wassily Kandinsky (and if Melanie Smith's 2010 film *Xilitla* suggests echoes of the work of Robert Smithson or Dan Flavin), might we also recognise the gaping divested architectures and apertures of Gordon Matta-Clark; the minimal abstractions of James Turrell or

Donald Judd; the inaccessibility of Michael Heiser's own city complex in the desert? We might think that the pavilions of Las Pozas possess status as temples, especially given their context in the landscape of a Mayan and Aztec heritage perhaps less prominent than that of James's Europe. Extending a role from early garden design, the constellation of pavilions, might serve to distribute myths and narratives around the landscape, moving subjects around on vertical and horizontal axes, in disorientating involutions of constructed and natural space.

If there is dialogue between horizontal and vertical in James's 'pavilion-stacks', the predominantly celebratory, upward gestures of Las Pozas might be usefully contrasted with those of the near-forgotten early Futurist artist and writer, Gilbert Clavel. Plagued by ill health, Clavel recuperated and settled in Positano on the east coast of Italy in 1919. With the help of local builders and his artisan friend Enrico Lietz, Clavel began to convert a 16th-century Saracen watchtower on the cliffs between Sorrento and Amalfi into a private underworld. Instead of building up and out, Clavel burrowed down into the rock, blasting out chambers with dynamite. Obsessed by ancient Egypt, mineralogy and mythology, Clavel had wild plans for his subterranean network, including converting a natural cavern into a vast egg-shaped concert hall, relating its form to his own removed testicle.[10] All chambers in some way mirrored his disfigured body, as if the whole complex were an emblem of his desire to change his body for a new one. Noted critic and philosopher, Siegfried Kracauer, in a 1925 essay for the *Frankfurter Zeitung*, not only described Clavel's honeycomb of passages as *Gekröse* ('chitterlings' or 'mesenteries'), but claimed that the project had "nothing in common with human architecture".[11] Whilst both Clavel's excavations and James's light-filled constructions share a mixture of narcissism and nostalgia, even the "ornamental expression of a child", they also appear to share a feeling for architecture and landscape both apart from and entwined with human desire.[12] A sense of the combination of what is earthly and what is otherworldly is given in an image of the event that led James to expand his ark-like sanctuary for flora and fauna into an evolving exposition of concrete pavilions. In 1962, a freak frost and snowfall destroyed up to twenty thousand of the wild orchids James had gathered. Local people described their terror at the sight of 'ashes' falling from the skies. This suggests that the concrete forms of Las Pozas would emerge from a something like a post-apocalyptic, inhuman landscape. Perhaps this is part of the reason that the pavilions appear both ancient and futuristic, both ruined and renewed. A futile battle against mortality would in fact produce structures that were just as impermanent but on an entirely different timescale. When James wrote in *Reading into the Picture*, again musing on his composite city of 'Seclusia', "there is nothing like a great loss to fire new initiative", he already prefigured his transition from patron to artist.[13] When he then asked himself: "how can my city be (...) both united, fantastic, and retain the charm of the unselfconscious?" his answer would only come decades later in a constellation of pavilions subservient to no 'main' structure except the encroaching jungle itself.[14]

Notes

Artichoke House / George Charman

1. Junyk, Ihor (2013) 'Not Months But Moments: Ephemerality, Monumentality and the Pavilion in Ruins'. *Open Arts Journal*, Issue 2.
2. Lippman, Caro W. (1952) 'Certain Hallucinations Peculiar to Migraine' *Journal of Nervous and Mental Disease*, 116 (4), pp.346-51.
3. Kusunoki, Sharon-Michi (2007) 'Edward James, Architect of Surrealism' in Wood, Ghislaine (ed.) *Surreal Things: Surrealism and Design*. London: V&A Publications, pp.205-214.
4. Gray, John (2014) 'J. G. Ballard Five Years On – A Celebration' in *The Guardian*, 4th April 2014.
5. Ballard, J. G. (1979) *The Unlimited Dream Company*. London: Harper Collins.
6. Ibid.
7. Stevens, Anthony (2003) *Jung: A Very Short Introduction*. Oxford: Oxford University Press.
Illustrations
p.7 Nicholson, Christopher. Scale model of the redesign of Pantheon Facade (situated on the Purple Landing at West Dean College). Original design by James Wyatt (1772). Edward James Cultural Archive. Photograph: George Charman.
p.9 Family home of J. G. Ballard, Old Charlton Road, Shepperton, Surrey. Image: Google Streetview. <Accessed on: 15/08/2014>
p.10 Home of Carl Gustav Jung on the upper lake at Bullingen, Zurich (1957). Image: En.wikipedia.org/bollinggen_tower. <Accessed on 10/08/2014>

Both in Progress: Artichoke House and a Typology of Sculpture / Marsha Bradfield and Lucy Tomlins

1. Hirshhorn Museum (2014) 'Speculative Forms' <www.hirshhorn.si.edu/collection/speculative-forms> <accessed June 1, 2014>
2. Bourriaud, Nicolas (2002) *Relational Aesthetics*. Translated from French by Simon Pleasance and Fronza Woods. Dijon-Quetigny, France: les presses du reel. P.19
3. Ibid., p.16.
4. Beuys, Joseph (1993) 'Interview with Willoughby Sharp' in *Energy Plan for the Western Man – Joseph Beuys in America, '77-'92*. New York: Four Walls Eight Windows. P.87.
5. Charman, George (2014) <www.george-charman.co.uk> <accessed June 1, 2014>
6. Davey, Grenville (2014) 'Video Interview', available through <www.pangaeasculptorscentre.com>
7. Pernice, Manfred (2008) *Que-Sah*, Exhibition at Neues Museum State Museum for Art and Design, Nuremberg.
8. Jerrman, Luke (2014) 'Video Interview', available through <www.pangaeasculptorscentre.com>
9. Wilson, Richard (2013) 'Tea and a Slice of Reality with Richard Wilson', Event organised by Pangaea Sculptors' Centre.
10. Jerrman, Luke (2014) 'Interview' available through <www.pangaeasculptorscentre.com>.

Edward James and the Poetry of the Imagination / Sharon-Michi Kusunoki

1. Boyle, Patrick (1978) *The Secret Life of Edward James*. UK: ITV Films.

2. James, Edward (c. 1970) Letter from Edward James to the Trustees of The Edward James Foundation. Edward James Cultural Archive, West Dean.

3. Fonthill Abbey, sometimes referred to as Beckford's Folly, was built in the style of a 'Gothic revival country house' between 1796 and 1813 at Fonthill Gifford in Wiltshire, England. It was originally built to house Beckford's library and art collection but the majority of the structure has either collapsed or been destroyed.

4. Horace Walpole began building Strawberry Hill House, a Gothic Revival villa with the turrets and battlements of castles, and the arched windows and stained glass of Gothic cathedrals, in Twickenham, London in 1749. The final stage was completed in 1776.

5. Casson, Hugh (14th December 1939) Letter from Sir Hugh Casson to Edward James's Secretary. Edward James Cultural Archive, West Dean. This letter was uncovered in one of the suitcases removed from Monkton House after James's death and stored in the Tower Suite of his West Dean home. It is presumed that the sketch to which Casson refers is the sketch for 'The Artichoke House,' which in the sketch is referred to as a 'pavilion.'

6. Kusunoki, Sharon-Michi (1994) In conversation with John Warren, Architect.

7. *Snow White and The Seven Dwarfs* (1937) Directed by Cottrell, David; Hand, David; Jackson, Wilfred; Morey, Larry; Pearce, Perce & Sharpsteen, Ben. Los Angeles: Walt Disney Productions.

8. James, Edward (1951) Preface to *The First Volume*. Draft copy (unpublished). Edward James Family Archive, England.

9. Ferdinand Cheval was a French postman who, between 1879 and 1923, built *Le Palais Idéal* in Hauterives, France. The palace was an amalgamation of styles and was constructed from the stones Cheval had collected on his postal routes. The leader of the Surrealist movement, André Breton, posthumously declared Cheval to be a Surrealist.

10. Dalí, Salvador (1933) 'De la beauté terrifiant et comestible de l' architecture modern-style'. *Minotaure*, No. 3-4.

11. Carrington, Leonora (1977) *The Stone Door*. New York: St. Martin's Press.

12. Preface to *The First Volume*. Op. cit.

13. Urbiola, Xavier Guzmán, et al. (1986) The Never Ending Habitat, Mexico: Universidad Autonoma Metropolitana - Xochimilco Campus.

14. James, Edward (21st December 1962) Letter from Edward James to Leonora Carrington. Edward James Cultural Archive, West Dean.

15. Urbiola, Xavier Guzmán (1994) In conversation with Sir Hugh Casson.

16. Preface to *The First Volume*, Op. cit.

17. James, Edward (1940) *Reading into the Picture*. London: Duckworth Press

Illustrations

p.31 Monkton House dining room (c. 1935) Edward James Cultural Archive.

p.34 Nicholson, Christopher. 'Artichoke House' (1936) Watercolour sketch of the exterior. Edward James Cultural Archive

p.35 Nicholson, Christopher. 'Artichoke House' (1936-39) Design for interior of Artichoke House Edward James Cultural Archive

p.41 Warren, John (1984) Edward James's grave stone, St Roche's Arboretum at West Dean

Notes and Sketches / John Warren

Illustrations

p.43 Warren, John (2014) Re-sketched proposal for Edward James's grave slab in St Roche's Arboretum. Image: property of John Warren.

p.45 Warren, John (2014) Re-sketched proposal for the Globular Gallery at West Dean. In-situ image of the exterior. Conceived by Edward James and worked up with John Warren. Image: property of John Warren.

p.45 Warren, John (2014) Re-sketched proposal for the Globular Gallery at West Dean. Half cross-section through the Gallery. Conceived by Edward James and worked up with John Warren. Image: property of John Warren.

The Pavilions of Xilitla / David R J Stent

1. Robinson, Joel (2014) 'Introducing Pavilions: Big Worlds under Little Tents' in *Open Arts Journal*, Issue 2 (Winter 2013-14) <www.openartsjournal.org>

2. Critic Sylvia Lavin bemoans the fact that the art pavilions of Biennales and Fairs are no longer sites of visionary radicality, but are rather disconnected from any "advanced cultural and historical project" and reduced to "party décor". [Lavin, Sylvia (2012) 'Vanishing Points: The Contemporary Pavilion', *Artforum International,* 51.2 (October), pp.212-219.]

3. Curtis, Penelope (2008) *Patio and Pavilion: The Place of Sculpture in Modern Architecture.* London: Ridinghouse, p9.

4. James was carful to emphasise that he was not interested in establishing a collection of Surrealist art, and that it 'accidentally' resulted from his intention to support living artists, giving them means to continue making work. This commitment to providing creative sanctuary carries over not only to Xilitla but also in his establishment of the Edward James Foundation and West Dean College in 1964 and 1971 respectively.

5. Hooks, Margaret (2007) *Surreal Eden: Edward James and Las Pozas.* New York: Princeton Architectural Press, p.16.

6. James, Edward (1940) *Reading into the Picture.* London: Duckworth Press, xix.

7. Ibid. xiv.

8. A comment made in Patrick Boyle's documentary *The Secret Life of Edward James* (1978) UK: ITV Films.

9. Op. cit. James, Edward (1940), xvii.

10. Cf. Tanaka, Jun (2012) 'The Chthonic Architecture of Gilbert Clavel: A Study of the Relationship among Architectural, Geographical, and Bodily Imagination'. Tokyo: Misuzu Shobo.

11. Kracauer, Siegfried (1987) 'Felsenwahn in Positano' ('Cliff Folly in Positano') in *Straßen in Berlin und anderswo.* Frankfurt am Main: Das Arenal, p.49.

12. Reeh, Henrick (2004) (trans. Irons, J.) *Ornaments of the Metropolis: Siegfried Kracauer and Modern Urban Culture.* Cambridge, MA: MIT Press, p.145.

13. Op. cit. James, Edward (1940), xiv.

14. Ibid., xviii.

Artichoke House / George Charman

September 6th - November 30th 2014

West Dean College
The Edward James Foundation
West Dean, Nr. Chichester, West Sussex PO18 0QZ

Support for the project was provided by:
Arts Council England's 'Grants for the Arts', The Edward James
Foundation and West Dean College's Artist in Residence programme.

Artichoke House was fabricated off-site by PiP Partnerships.
info@pippartnership.com
www.pippartnership.com

Tel: +44 (0)1243 811301
Email: reception@westdean.org.uk
www.westdean.org.uk

58